PERSONAL PERFORMANCE CONTRACTS
The Key to Job Success

Roger Fritz

CRISP PUBLICATIONS, INC.
Los Altos, California

PERSONAL PERFORMANCE CONTRACTS:
The Key to Job Success

English language Crisp books are distributed worldwide. Our major international distributors include:

CANADA: Reid Publishing, LTD., Box 7267, Oakville, Ontario Canada L6J 6L6. TEL: (416) 842-4428, FAX: (416) 842-9327

AUSTRALIA: Career Builders, P. O. Box 1051, Springwood, Brisbane, Queensland, Australia 4127. TEL: 841-1061, FAX: 841-1580

NEW ZEALAND: Career Builders, P. O. Box 571, Manurewa, Auckland, New Zealand. TEL: 266-5276, FAX: 266-4152

JAPAN: Phoenix Associates Co., Mizuho Bldg. 2-12-2, Kami Osaki, Shinagawa-Ku, Tokyo 141, Japan. TEL: 3-443-7231, FAX: 3-443-7640

Selected Crisp titles are also available in other languages. Contact International Rights Manager Tim Polk at (415) 949-4888 for more information.

CREDITS
Editor: **Michael Crisp**
Designer: **Carol Harris**
Typesetting: **Interface Studio**
Cover Design: **Carol Harris**

Copyright © 1987 by Crisp Publications, Inc.
Library of Congress Catalog Card Number 85-73466
Fritz, Roger
Personal Performance Contracts
ISBN 0-931961-12-2

FOR KATE — WHO ACCEPTED
THE BEST CONTRACT I EVER MADE

ABOUT THIS BOOK

PERSONAL PERFORMANCE CONTRACTS: THE KEY TO JOB SUCCESS is not like most books. It has a unique "self-paced" format that encourages a reader to become personally involved. Designed to be "read with a pencil," there is an abundance of exercises, activities, assessments and cases that invite participation.

The objective of PERSONAL PERFORMANCE CONTRACTS is to help a manager learn what a Personal Performance Contract is; why it is a fundamental skill of management; and how to complete one in a professional manner. Managers can then make any required behavioral changes applying concepts presented in the book to their unique management situation.

PERSONAL PERFORMANCE CONTRACTS (and the other self-improvement books listed on page 71) can be used effectively in a number of ways. Here are some possibilities:

— Individual Study. Because the book is self-instructional, all that is needed is a quiet place, some time and a pencil. By completing the activities and exercises, a manager should not only receive valuable feedback, but also practical ideas about steps for self-improvement.

— Workshops and Seminars. The book is ideal for pre-assigned reading prior to a workshop or seminar. With the basics in hand, the quality of the participation should improve. More time can be spent on concept extensions and applications during the program. The book can also be effective when a trainer distributes it at the beginning of a session, and leads participants through the contents.

— Remote Location Training. Copies can be sent to those not able to attend "home office" training sessions.

There are other possibilities that depend on the objectives, program or ideas of the user. One thing for sure, even after it has been read, this book will serve as excellent reference material which can be easily reviewed. Good luck!

YOU AND THE PPC*

TO THE MANAGER OR TRAINER—

PERSONAL PERFORMANCE CONTRACTS has been prepared to meet two needs: (1) Self study, and (2) Group training. The ideas presented in this book are workable; and the methods recommended have been proven on the job.

For group training the following is recommended:

> Introduce and discuss, "Where Are You Now?",
>   pp. 2-10, first hour.
> Introduce and discuss, "Preparing the Performance Contract,"
>   pp. 11-28, one hour.
> Introduce and discuss, "Action Needed to Produce Results,"
>   pp. 29-37, one hour.
> Discuss, "Introducing the Personal Performance Contract,"
>   pp. 38-50, one hour.
> Discuss the step-by-step process,
>   pp. 51-60, one hour.
> Critique "Your Personal Performance Contract,"
>   p. 61, one hour.

The six hours of training can be accomplished in a single day, (with breaks at mid-morning, mid-afternoon, and lunch), or done effectively in two half-day sessions.

The essence of the Personal Performance Contract is a recorded agreement between individuals. Each person should feel "ownership" in an agreement before any written document is made final.

During group training it is recommended that the trainer spend time with each individual in order to maximize the benefits.

Remember—good intentions are not enough. Lasting improvement comes only when we know what is expected and deliberately set a course to achieve it. A Personal Performance Contract is the most simple and direct way to give meaning to personal goals <u>and</u> accomplish company priorities. This means employees must be active participants. Once this has been accomplished the benefits will repay your efforts to implement PPC's many times over.

—Roger Fritz

*PPC—Personal Performance Contract

YOU AND THE PPC*

TO THE READER—

"If you don't know where you're going, any road will take you there!"

How important is performance to you? To your organization?

This book deals with the basic essentials of achieving success at work. Success has nothing to do with luck, or being at the right place at the right time; or knowing the right person. These can help but success is achieved by those who know how to prepare for it. At work this means a deliberate method of determining <u>who</u> will do <u>what</u>, by <u>when</u>.

PERSONAL PERFORMANCE CONTRACTS sets the stage for performance. It enables supervisors and employees to jointly prepare and commit to agreements. Performance Contracts cement job commitments. Once parties become obligated to each other, performance should improve because accountability has been established and agreed upon.

My objective will have been met when you put the simple and direct principles in this book to work for you.

—Roger Fritz

*PPC—Personal Performance Contract

> The most important question for <u>all</u> employees, at <u>all</u> times, under <u>all</u> circumstances is–What do we mean by performance?

CONTENTS

CONTENTS

A Chinese proverb tells us that the longest journey must begin with a single step, and Marie Edmond Jones said, "The way to begin is to begin."

Regardless of your experience as a manager or supervisor, it is important that you know what Personal Performance Contracts are; why they are important; and how to construct one that will achieve significant results. This book will help you accomplish these objectives. For openers, it is important to discover where you are now.

WHERE ARE YOU NOW?

Here are some important questions to determine where you are now...
Answer each question honestly:

DO YOU CURRENTLY HAVE SPECIFIC WRITTEN PERFORMANCE
PRIORITIES OR STANDARDS AGAINST WHICH IT IS POSSIBLE TO
MEASURE YOUR ACHIEVEMENT?

( ) YES ( ) NO

DO YOUR SUPERVISOR/EMPLOYEES KNOW ABOUT THEM?

( ) YES ( ) NO

DO YOU REGULARLY CONFIRM YOUR PRIORITIES AND STANDARDS
IN ORDER TO REMAIN ON TARGET?

( ) YES ( ) NO

ARE YOUR ON-THE-JOB PRIORITIES SUFFICIENTLY FLEXIBLE TO
MEET NEW DEMANDS OR UNEXPECTED CHANGES IN THE
DIRECTION OF WORK?

( ) YES ( ) NO

ARE YOU BASICALLY SATISFIED THAT YOU AND/OR YOUR
PEOPLE ARE MAKING MEASURABLE PROGRESS TOWARD
ESTABLISHED WORK GOALS?

( ) YES ( ) NO

IS IT LIKELY YOUR SUPERIORS/SUBORDINATES WOULD AGREE?

( ) YES ( ) NO

ARE YOU CONFIDENT YOUR ESTABLISHED PRIORITIES ARE
CONTRIBUTING TO THE GROWTH OF YOUR ORGANIZATION?

( ) YES ( ) NO

<u>Regardless of How You Answered The Questions on Page 3:</u>

You should realize that performance priorities aren't about run-of-the-mill daily chores. They're expected. They keep the engine running. But their top speed is only second gear.

Performance priorities discussed in this book must meet certain criteria. They must:

 * Be important enough to create some excitement or enthusiasm and stimulate extra effort

 * Be challenging enough so results will bring rewards that outweigh the effort required to achieve them.

 * Cover a long enough time to accommodate short-range setbacks and disappointments

---

The best method for achieving outstanding performance, meeting objectives and insuring appropriate recognition is to prepare and use PERSONAL PERFORMANCE CONTRACTS!

PERSONAL PERFORMANCE CONTRACTS: A DEFINITION

WHAT IS A PERSONAL PERFORMANCE CONTRACT? (PPC)

In simplest terms, a PERSONAL PERFORMANCE CONTRACT is a **WRITTEN AGREEMENT** between an employee and his or her manager which **RECORDS ACCOMPLISHMENTS** to be achieved within a **SPECIFIC TIME PERIOD**. Accomplishments should have **BENEFITS** for the employee as well as for the organization.

Here are the basic steps to be taken when constructing a PPC agreement:

1. Engage in a careful job **analysis** to pinpoint the most important needs which are to be satisfied.

2. Prepare **objectives** for the highest priority needs identified in the analysis. Achievement of these objectives should be vital to success on that job.

3. Develop an **action plan** which specifies exactly who will be doing what by when.

4. Prepare a **time & cost schedule** to accurately measure the dollar impact of achievement within a specific time frame.

5. Emphasize **self-development** as an integral part of the agreement.

6. Conduct regular **reviews** to insure progress meets expectations.

> This description is equally true for your Personal Performance Contract as well as those who report to you.

Preparing and implementing an effective Performance Contract is never a routine chore–even for experienced people. It demands commitment, but also offers these significant benefits:

1. A unique opportunity to view the job from two important view points–that of the boss <u>and</u> the employee.

2. A method by which to agree on needs and identify priorities.

3. A format that allows continual concentration on objectives.

4. A chance for the employee to see the "big picture", and better understand any changes that occur.

5. A clearer focus on those problems and/or obstacles that require a solution.

6. A means to pinpoint accountability for action, (<u>who</u> will do <u>what</u> by <u>when</u>?).

(THE NEXT PAGE MAY BE REPRODUCED WITHOUT PRIOR PERMISSION. COPIES SHOULD BE GIVEN TO EACH PERSON FOR COMPLETION.)

SUCCESS DEFINED*

Complete the following activity. Prepare as complete a list as possible.
See the next page for a comparison of ideas.

A SUCCESSFUL EMPLOYEE IS ONE WHO:

SUCCESS FOR ME PERSONALLY MEANS:

SUCCESS IN MY JOB DEPENDS ON MY ABILITY TO:

MY FORMULA FOR ACHIEVING SUCCESS IS:

Definitions of success will be as different as the number of people involved. Successful people, however, have several common characteristics. These include:

* An ability to stand on one's own feet.

* Courage to assume responsibility for decisions that are made.

* The ability to set some personal development goals.

* A willingness to pursue what is "right."

Successful people also understand that growth is natural and change is part of growth.

Ask those who work with you to consider things about themselves that are truly unique. Those skills and characteristics that make them feel confident and proficient. Then ask them to consider how they can best apply their talents.

DO YOU KNOW YOUR STRENGTHS?

EVALUATING EMPLOYEES' STRENGTHS*/ EVALUATING YOUR STRENGTHS

1. MOST ASPECTS OF MY JOB REALLY TURN ME ON.

   (   ) YES   (   ) NO

2. I HAVE PERSONAL GROWTH OBJECTIVES EVEN IF NOT FORMALLY REQUIRED.

   (   ) YES   (   ) NO

3. THE CONTRIBUTIONS I MAKE ARE VALUED BY MY COMPANY.

   (   ) YES   (   ) NO

4. I AM WILLING TO ACCEPT ACCOUNTABILITY AND RESPONSIBILITY FOR MY JOB ACTIONS AND DECISIONS.

   (   ) YES   (   ) NO

5. I HAVE LEARNED FROM PAST MISTAKES AND FAILURES.

   (   ) YES   (   ) NO

6. I TRY TO MAKE FULL USE OF MY KNOWLEDGE AND EXPERIENCE WHILE ON THE JOB.

   (   ) YES   (   ) NO

NOW TURN THE PAGE AND COMPARE YOUR ANSWERS. BE SURE YOUR EMPLOYEES ALSO COMPLETE THIS EXERCISE AND REVIEW THEIR ANSWERS WITH THEM INDIVIDUALLY.

*Ask those preparing a PPC to complete this activity.

AUTHOR'S RESPONSE

1. IF YOU ANSWERED "NO," take a hard look at your job. You might be happier in another position. If you basically like what you do, try handling some of your routines in a new, more creative way. Test your originality. Read for new ideas. Talk with colleagues on ways they stay motivated. Experiment for better results.

2. IF YOU ANSWERED "YES," you have discovered that the key to success lies in creating meaningful targets to shoot for, and that satisfaction comes when these targets are achieved.

3. IF YOUR ANSWER WAS "NO," ask yourself if you are utilizing all the knowledge, skills and experience garnered over the years. How do you view the potential within your current job? How about your boss? Do you get enough feedback from her or him on the value of your contributions?

4. IF YOU CHECKED "YES" to this question, congratulations! It's obvious you have self-confidence. You also probably recognize that everyone has moments when they feel inadequate. You understand that risking a mistake is better than doing nothing.

5. IF YOU ANSWERED "NO," you have missed a great learning experience. Disappointments should not defeat you. Study your mistakes to avoid similar problems in the future. Maintain an optimistic outlook. Failures have a way of stretching your abilities.

6. A "NO" ANSWER SUGGESTS you may not have clearly defined what is essential to your advancement. Do you fight change or use it as a step forward? Are you committed to an ideal? An action? A challenge?

KEYS TO JOB SUCCESS

The previous exercise should suggest existing opportunities you and/or your people may have overlooked. Certainly what has been revealed indicates an opening for a more creative use of talent.

Successful people in business are motivated by many things. We all can identify money, status or power, but there is another dimension: namely satisfaction. Truly successful people are determined to do a good job; make a contribution; or advance their business or profession for the personal satisfaction that comes from a job well done.

THE KEY TO JOB SUCCESS LIES IN A PLANNED, SUSTAINED EFFORT. ONE OF THE EASIEST MEANS TO INSURE THIS SUCCESS RESTS WITH A CAREFULLY THOUGHT OUT PERFORMANCE CONTRACT BETWEEN YOU AND YOUR BOSS—AS WELL AS BETWEEN YOU AND THE PEOPLE WHO REPORT TO YOU.

The balance of this book will explain how to develop a quality Personal Performance Contract.

CASE STUDIES

Case studies provide insights about the content being introduced.

The first case (on the facing page) can help you better understand the importance of reviewing job specifications before beginning the selection process.

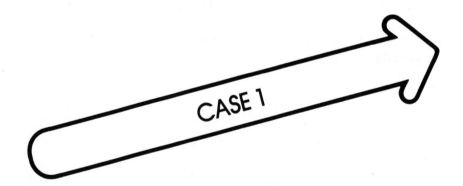

CASE 1

CASE 1

DIFFICULT CHOICES

Harry Phillips just completed his first year as Manager. He is a good performer, but his main problem is dealing with people. He supervises six people, most of whom had been peers. One of his subordinates, Production Supervisor Joe Jefferson, is four years from retirement. Joe is in good health, competent and friendly, but works at a very relaxed pace. Harry had done little about this because he had no clear-cut idea about how to motivate Joe. In fact, Harry has found the situation embarrassing because although he likes supervising, he hates dealing with problems like Joe's lack of productivity. He realizes he has a tendency to avoid these problems rather than face them.

Another problem in Harry's department is Jim Thomas, his Engineering Supervisor. Jim is about Harry's age. Everyone knows that Jim wanted the job Harry received. Jim felt he deserved the promotion instead of Harry. Since Harry's promotion, Jim has been polite when dealing with Harry, however his work has fallen off significantly both in quantity and quality. Harry had not talked to Jim about this, even though it is noticeable to everyone. It seems to Harry that the problem is getting worse because the two young engineers who work with Jim are also slacking off. The younger men complain frequently to Harry about how little Joe and Jim are accomplishing.

A. How could a Personal Performance Contract help Harry deal with Joe and Jim?

B. What key result areas should Joe's personal PPC include?

C. What key result areas should Jim's PPC include?

D. How much time would you allow for the benefits of the PPC to become evident?

(See Author's responses on page 67).

PREPARING THE PERFORMANCE CONTRACT

A recent study conducted by industrial psychologists summarized the attitudes of over 200,000 employees toward their companies. ·

The results?

More than half took a dim view of their workplace and their company.

A majority resented the way layoffs were handled.

Most felt there was too great a difference in pay between supervisors and those supervised.

Almost half questioned the integrity of management.

Sixty percent lacked confidence in their company's future.

Most worried because they had so little say about decisions which affected their future.

It's time to start setting performance goals for the next quarter.

DO YOUR EMPLOYEES...

UNDERSTAND conditions faced by your company in the marketplace, including the strength of competitors and the resulting effect on company policies and procedures?

DEVELOP specific, achievable, realistic objectives for their own jobs—objectives that can measurably move the company forward?

PREPARE action plans to insure the kind of consistent results required for success?

REMAIN alert for problems and obstacles that need to be resolved or eliminated before progress can be made?

RELATE their personal performance to objectives that the company expects to accomplish?

THE COMMON DENOMINATOR OF ALL THE ABOVE IS THE FOUNDATION OF THE PERSONAL PERFORMANCE CONTRACT! Your first step is on the next page.

STEP 1
COMPLETE A JOB ANALYSIS WORKSHEET

Employees need to understand their job and where they are headed before good decisions can be made. Like taking a trip, you must know where you are going before you decide how to prepare for your journey and how to get on the right road.

To conduct a realistic evaluation of your present situation involves similar planning. You must ORGANIZE FACTS AND DETERMINE POSSIBLE COURSES OF ACTION.

To do this, you (and/or your employees) should complete a job analysis worksheet similar to the one on the following page. It will help answer questions such as:

* Is the information about my job accurate and complete?

* Do I have a current job description or set of job objectives?

* Have I prioritized the key results expected in order to concentrate on items that deserve the most attention?

* Am I aware of any trends that may require changes in procedure, or indicate a potential danger.

* Have I considered new ways to approach my job that can save time, effort and/or money?

FOLLOWING ARE SOME OF THE MORE PRODUCTIVE INFORMATION SOURCES FOR YOU AND/OR YOUR EMPLOYEES.

* Past Performance Analysis
* Key memos/letters/directives
* Pertinent company reports
* Quotas/budgets/forecasts
* Job-related coaching/counseling/training sessions

ADD ANY ADDITIONAL SOURCES THAT COULD BE USEFUL.

JOB ANALYSIS WORKSHEET

CHECKPOINTS	FACTS/INFORMATION AFFECTING JOB PERFORMANCE	TIMING/IDEAS/ SUGGESTIONS TO INCLUDE IN CONTRACT
JOB PURPOSE What is the major purpose of my job? • What KNOWLEDGE is required? (marketing, customers, economics, etc.) • What SKILLS are necessary? (problem-solving, writing, decision-making, salesmanship, etc.) • What TRAITS are needed? (self-confidence, empathy, aggressiveness, etc.) What was I REALLY hired to accomplish? Do I have a true sense of the way things WORK in this company? What RESOURCES from the company are available to me? Am I taking full advantage of them? RESPONSIBILITIES In what areas am I STRONGEST? WEAKEST? How well do I organize my TIME? DUTIES? Other job ACTIVITIES? PERFORMANCE Do I know what PRIORITIES are most important to the company? How well do I IMPLEMENT them?	EDUCATION/EXPERIENCE What can I offer in the way of education/experience/expertise not now available from other people in the company? COMMUNICATION SKILLS How well do I communicate to subordinates? Peers? Supervisors? Other departments? COOPERATION What degree of rapport have I established with other departments within the company? BIG PICTURE Am I aware of key company priorities? How well do I help implement them? PAST PERFORMANCE How do those with whom I work feel about my job performance? What about supervisors? Peers? BUDGET ANALYSIS Am I able to keep operating costs within budget? Have I pointed out areas to my supervisor in which savings are possible?	When and under what circumstances should the contract be presented? Does information in the contract answer most of the questions my boss is likely to ask? What parts of the contract should be communicated to my peers? Subordinates? Others? Have all explanations been presented for additional costs, or other changes to the current work environment ?

(USE THE BLANK WORKSHEET ON THE NEXT PAGES TO DO YOUR OWN JOB ANALYSIS.)

JOB ANALYSIS WORKSHEET*

CHECKPOINTS	FACTS/INFORMATION AFFECTING JOB PERFORMANCE	TIMING/IDEAS/ SUGGESTIONS TO INCLUDE IN CONTRACT
JOB PURPOSE		
RESPONSIBILITIES		
PERFORMANCE		

*This sheet may be reproduced without permission of the publisher.

JOB ANALYSIS WORKSHEET*

CHECKPOINTS	FACTS/INFORMATION AFFECTING JOB PERFORMANCE	TIMING/IDEAS/ SUGGESTIONS TO INCLUDE IN CONTRACT
JOB PURPOSE		
RESPONSIBILITIES		
PERFORMANCE		

*This sheet may be reproduced without permission of the publisher

STEP 2	SELECT PRIORITY OBJECTIVES

A careful look at the Job Analysis Worksheet just completed should help identify the highest priority goals to use in your performance contract.

Following are three categories of performance:

1. Job Routines that need improvement. (Daily chores such as preparation of reports; customer service; quality control; training, etc.). Although "routine" they are too important to be considered trivial. They are the lubricant that keep the business functioning smoothly. When the basics are understood and controlled more important new objectives can be pursued.

2. Problems That Need To Be Solved. People who learn to become problem solvers have special value to their organizations. Problem-solvers resolve a lack of progress by taking a results-oriented approach.

3. Innovations For Added Benefits. Those capable of providing true job innovations are the "champions." This special group takes positive action that provides creative breakthroughs.

INDIVIDUAL AND ORGANIZATION OBJECTIVES

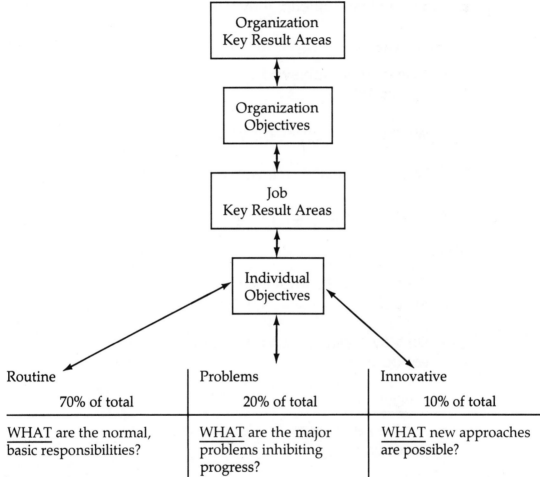

Routine	Problems	Innovative
70% of total	20% of total	10% of total
WHAT are the normal, basic responsibilities?	WHAT are the major problems inhibiting progress?	WHAT new approaches are possible?
• How well are these currently being handled?	• How much improvement is realistic?	• What are the added benefits?
• What activities require the most time?	• What immediate actions suggest themselves?	• How about costs?
• How prone are they to delegation?	• Who is qualified to take them on?	• What checks/balances are required?
• Are trained people involved?	• How long should it take?	• How long before results will be known?

THREE IMPORTANT CRITERIA

The priority objectives you select (page 20) should meet three criteria. They must be:

1. <u>REASONABLE:</u>
   - Can they be achieved in the time available?

   - Will they bring about desired changes?

   - Will costs be within allowable budgets?

   - Will they create new problems?

2. <u>SPECIFIC:</u>
   - Do they specify what the improvements will be?

   - Do they explain when results can be expected?

3. <u>AMBITIOUS:</u>
   - Are they sufficiently challenging and rewarding?

   - Will they resolve problems and/or seize new opportunities?

   - If implemented, will they be profitable?

THE CONCEPT OF KEY RESULT AREAS

<u>What is a Key Result Area?</u>

A prevailing attitude among those who hesitate to commit themselves to performance contracts is the belief that it is not possible to measure the work they perform. This is heard more frequently from those who deal with intangibles, such as values, or services, as compared to those whose jobs involve manufactured items, or sales quotas.

Some jobs are more difficult to measure than others, but none are impossible to measure. The problem is reduced greatly when a job is broken into its component parts. Separate responsibilities or duties can be itemized. These distinct job parts are called <u>key result areas</u>. They are not goals, but areas of responsibility from which specific goals can be prepared. A key result area answers the questions: ''What are the things I am accountable for?'' ''What are the major component parts of my job?''

For example:

KEY RESULT AREA FOR BILL JONES

1. Responsible for all production schedules

2. Responsible for finished product quality control

3. Responsible for safety in production department

4. _____

PRIMARY NEEDS BY KEY RESULT AREA

1. Back order delays are causing some loss of customer business

2. Quality has fallen below the 96% acceptable target

3. Lost time due to accidents has increased 8% during past 6 months

4. _____

The best way to eliminate disagreement and conflict over what was accomplished is to determine in advance how progress will be measured. Indicators are best expressed in terms of Quality, Quantity, Time and Cost.

HOW CAN PROGRESS BE MEASURED?

(Examples of Progress Indicators)

QUANTITY	Number of customers/clients served per month...quarter...etc.
	Number items processed (orders, forms) per week...month...etc.
	Average backlog of orders per day...month...etc.
	Number cases handled (referrals, complaints) per quarter...etc.
	Number of customer complaints per year...etc.
	% employee participation (in specific programs)
	Number person hours lost to absenteeism per quarter...etc.
QUALITY	Error rate/ratio (by department...project...etc.)
	Production hours lost due to injury (severity rate) per quarter...year...etc.
	% orders without error
	Rate of employee turnover
	% tests repeated
	% work redone (or rejected completely)
	% time out of order (downtime) or unproductive
TIME	# or % deadlines missed
	# or % answered within 5 days
	# of days to complete
	# of working days after end of month/quarter
	Time elapsed (turn-around time)
	Frequency each month/quarter
COST	% variance from budget
	$ as line item in budget (e.g., overtime)
	Dollars saved over previous period/quarter
	$ cost per person contact or order received
	# hours to complete each time

Use the sample worksheet on the next page as a guide.

SAMPLE

Progress Indicator Worksheet for Betsy Stevens, Production Supervisor

KEY RESULT AREA	% Importance	Measures Quantity/Quality/Time/Cost
Cost Control	25%	# written bid specifications?
		% competitive bids on components?
		deadline met for 3% expense reduction?
		stayed within total budget?
Production Scheduling	40%	# or % schedules met?
		# or % on-time shipments?
		deadlines missed by product?
Quality Control	20%	$ value of wasted material?
		$ value of product recalled?
		# or type of customer complaints?
Safety	15%	# accidents?
		classified by severity?
		downtown?
		insurance costs?

100%

NOW YOU TRY IT

Progress Indicators Worksheet* For _____
                                            Name

KEY RESULT AREA	% Importance	Measures Quantity/Quality/Time/Cost
	100%	

*This sheet may be copied without further permission of the publisher.

KEY QUESTIONS

After determining the key result areas (normally 4 or 5 for each job), and the most important current need for each area, (review page 23); the next step is to schedule a meeting to insure there is agreement between an employee and his/her manager on questions such as:

• Why are listed needs important?

• What key results are expected?

• What are the potential obstacles?

• What is the organization's performance target?

• How will progress be measured in terms of quality, quantity, time & cost?

• What is the action plan for accountability–<u>Who</u> will be doing <u>what</u> by <u>when</u>?

The facing page shows a sample of how a personal performance analysis will lead from the general to the specific as each question is answered.

SAMPLE

PERSONAL PERFORMANCE CONTRACT WORKSHEET

Key Result Area	Need	Why Important	How Important %	Potential Obstacles	Performance Targets/Results Expected	Measures Quality/Quantity Time, Cost	Action Plan (Who, What, When)
Cost Control	Reduce departmental expenses by 15% during 2nd quarter	Profits must be improved	25%	Vendor prices too high & competition limited	Bid costs on all components — Locate minimum of three new suppliers	% improvement upon completion	Jim T. propose bid specs by 4/10 John T. Approve by 4/15 Frank O. implement by 5/20
Production Scheduling	Reduce backorder delays to 3 work days	Losing key customers	40%	Cost of new equipment Employee resistence	Automate component assembly on line 1 & 2 by 9/1	Deadline missed by product % customers retained Startup date met?	Jane N.—prepare report by 5/1 Max R.—approve plan by 5/12 Joe P.—complete automation project by 6/30
Supplies	Stock outages delaying shipments	Lost 4 customers last month with total orders of $185,000	15%	Unreliable vendors No inspections in receiving dept.	Get new vendors Assign inspector to receiving dept.	# days to complete # customers regained % shipment rejected $ value of shipments delayed	Nancy G.—get new vendor by 4/20 Tom H.—select and train new inspector by 4/30
Security	Eliminate employee theft	Inventory loss was $55,000 last quarter	10%	Most material is in unrestricted storage areas	Reduce inventory loss by 50% in 3 months	# incidents of theft $ amount of missing material	Susan M.—recommend action by 4/1 Jack C.—provide locked storage for priority materials by 4/15
Safety	Lost time due to accidents up 30% in 1st Qtr.	Insurance costs up 60% in past 2 years Paid time off increasing	10% / 100%	Finding a new insurance carrier Supervisors are indifferent	Reduce frequency rate by 10% this quarter Reduce severity rate by 12% this quarter	# & % of incident reports prepared next day Manhours lost Cost to correct unsafe conditions	Leslie B.—prepare weekly report beginning 4/1 Mark D.—recommend corrective action by 5/1 Sam S.—implement by 6/30

This contract is for the period _____ to _____ .
(mth/day/yr)   (mth/day/yr)

Signed _____

Signed _____
(supervisor)

Personal Performance Contracts

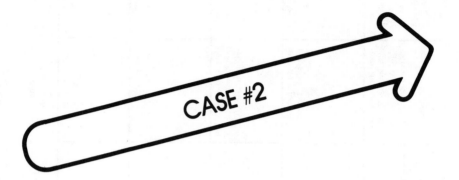

NOTE: For a highly regarded book on how to conduct an effective performance appraisal, see page 69.

WHAT WOULD YOU DO?

It was seven p.m. and the office had been closed for two hours, but Sue Fleming was still at her desk. She was finishing a report due the next morning. Although she normally enjoyed preparing such reports, she was annoyed with herself for not taking a stronger stand when information for the report was turned in half-finished by Mary Keller, one of her employees. If this had been the only time that Mary had turned in unfinished work Sue would not have been angry. The problem was that Mary did this regularly. On several occasions Sue's schedule had been set back completing a design proposal which was Mary's responsibility.

Management textbooks call Mary's action, ''delegating upward.'' The first step recommended by a textbook to deal with the problem is to confront the employee. Sue doesn't want to do that. None of Mary's previous supervisors complained about her performance, and Sue doesn't want to call attention to a problem that might somehow be her fault. Besides, she thought, staying late once in a while isn't the end of the world.

A. What effect is the situation likely to have on Sue?

B. What effect is this situation likely to have on Mary?

C. How would you deal with this situation if you were Sue?

D. How would you introduce a PPC to Mary?

Compare your thoughts with those of the author on page 67.

STEP 3

COMMIT TO AN ACTION PLAN
TO ACHIEVE RESULTS

Many people hesitate to commit to a plan, because they feel it is not possible to assess what they do because of varied responsibilities and a complex job.

Some jobs are more difficult to assess than others, but every job can be measured. Yet, even with a good measurement system, little is likely to happen unless specific accountability is assigned for each step.

Objectives tell how much progress needs to be made, and where to concentrate. An action plan describes who will do what by when.

A step by step method to build a solid action plan is presented on the next five pages.

BUILDING AN ACTION PLAN

Following are items which a good Action Plan should contain. It should:

DESIGNATE who is required to carry the plan to success;

DETAIL what activity or equipment is needed to achieve the planned objectives;

SPECIFY when checkpoints need to be met; and

DETERMINE which alternative courses of action should be available.

Careful preparation is essential if the performance contract is to achieve the results expected. Properly done, a thoughtful action plan will provide these indirect benefits:

1. Time management will improve because:
   - There is agreement where to concentrate.
   - Low priority activities can be dropped or reassigned.
   - There will be fewer "false starts" or changes in direction.

2. Teamwork will improve because key players have a common game plan;

3. Rate and severity of errors will decrease;

4. There will be fewer excuses because of assigned accountability.

AFTER REVIEWING THE
PLANNING FORMAT
CAREFULLY, EACH EMPLOYEE
SHOULD COMPLETE A FORM
SIMILAR TO THE ONE ON THE
FACING PAGE. THEN THE
COMPLETED FORM SHOULD
BE REVIEWED BY THE
APPROPRIATE
SUPERVISOR/MANAGER.

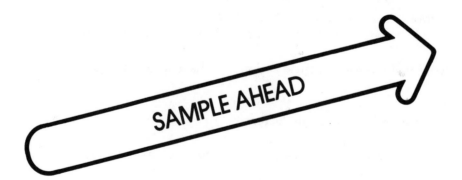

SAMPLE AHEAD

ACTION PLAN SAMPLE

OBJECTIVES & PLANS OF ACTION

Dept: BUSINESS OFFICE	Prepared By:	Date: 2-2-	Page 1 of 1 Pages
Position: SUPERVISOR			

OBJECTIVES & RESULTS to be accomplished:
(SPECIFIC RESULTS)
WHAT · WHEN · WHERE
and
NET COST-BENEFIT

Objective #1 of 5 Weight 25%

WHAT

Develop a micro-fiche system for all itemized bills to eliminate preparation, matching, in-filing, out-filing and microfilming of 4000 records p/month

WHEN

To be operational by 3/1

WHERE

At Headquarters

NET COST BENEFIT

Estimated savings of $30,000 p/year

Distribution to:

HOW (TO ACCOMPLISH IT)	When-To Be Done (Schedule)	Who-is To Do It (Assgm't)	Approved By	Status & Dates
1. Realign registration procedures.				
A. Prepare procedures and flow charts covering the new system.	2-4	R.S. S.S.	C.Z. W.B.	
B. Train clerks to phase out the preparation of old folders and put new system into effect.	2-15	S.S.	R.S.	
C. Discontinue preparation of old folders—in out-patient registration department.	2-15	S.S.	R.S.	
D. Maintain a file of registration forms—and deliver to all supervisors.	2-14	S.S.	R.S.	
2. Realign the file room procedures.				
A. Prepare procedures and flow charts—covering the file room procedures	2-6	L.A. R.S.	C.Z. W.B.	
B. Train file room staff—in micro-fiche systems and procedures	2-10	L.A.	R.S.	
C. Check bills—for accuracy and completeness.	2-11	L.A.	R.S.	
D. Maintain a file of bills—and deliver to supervisor.	2-10	L.A.	R.S.	
E. Preparation of new folders.	2-14	L.A.	R.S.	

Reviewed By:

Position:

Dates:

Follow Up:

Write each Objective and Plan of Action on a separate page

Without an action plan, goals are merely good intentions. **Action Plans** are necessary to pin down accountability. They determine <u>Who</u> will do <u>What</u> by <u>When</u>.

Following the example on page 35, you should now be ready to prepare an **Action Plan** for one of your highest priority objectives. Use a pencil so you can readily make changes. Be sure to answer these important questions:

–Is the objective really worth accomplishing? Will it make a significant difference when completed?

–Will completing it be cost-effective?

–Do I know the financial impact? Is it significant? Would my boss agree?

–Have the necessary steps been determined? Is the sequence proper?

–Have the right people been informed? Involved?

–Are the deadlines realistic?

–Are the interim checkpoints acceptable?

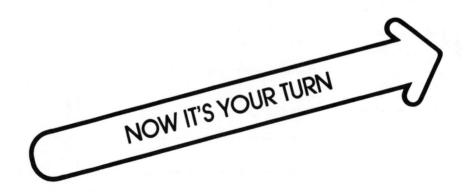

NOW IT'S YOUR TURN

Personal Performance Contracts

Write one objective and Plan of Action on this page.

NAME _____

POSITION _____

PAGE ____ OF ____

DATE ____

OBJECTIVES & RESULTS (SPECIFIC RESULTS to be accomplished: WHAT WHEN WHERE and NET COST-BENEFIT)	PLAN OF ACTION Sequenced, step-by-step action to take: HOW (TO ACCOMPLISH IT)	When-To Be Done (Schedule)	Who-is To Do It (Assgm't)	Approved By	Status & Dates
Objective # __ of __ Weight __ %					
WHAT					
WHEN					
WHERE					
NET COST BENEFIT					
Distribution to:					
Reviewed By:	Position:	Dates:	Follow Up:		

Write each Objective and Plan of Action on a separate page

To be effective in planning requires follow-up and flexibility. This means you must be prepared to modify or re-direct portions of your plan as situations dictate or conditions change.

To insure work loads are realistic a SCHEDULE is needed. This is nothing more than a regular means of keeping your plan functioning effectively. You need to:

1. Anticipate the amount of time required to meet deadlines

2. Determine if objectives are being achieved on schedule

3. Personally check any problem that causes a delay

4. Insure the project deadlines remain realistic, and

5. KEEP EVERYONE INFORMED OF PROGRESS!

SAMPLE AHEAD

NAME_____

REVIEW/REVISE WORKSHEET

OBJECTIVE NUMBER _____

MONTH	DATE	CHANGES REQUIRED IN OBJECTIVES/PLAN
January	1st Monday	Bid specs not accurate; no input from legal department
February	3rd Monday	Revised bid specs sent on 1/25 (6 days late)
March	3rd Monday	Low bid still $85,000 over projected cost
April	1st Monday	Specs rewritten and approved on 3/20 (35 days late)
May	1st Monday	3 new bidders solicited
May	3rd Monday	New bid accepted ($65,000 under previous low bid)
June	2nd Monday	Contract signed (55 days later than original goal)

PREPARE THE BLANK REVIEW/REVISE
WORKSHEET ON THE FACING PAGE FOR
EACH OF YOUR KEY OBJECTIVES.

CHECK INDIVIDUAL WORKSHEETS TO SEE IF
THEY SUPPORT YOUR PERSONAL PLANNING
EFFORTS.

DO IT NOW

NAME_____ *

REVIEW/REVISE WORKSHEET

OBJECTIVE NUMBER _____

MONTH	DATE	CHANGES REQUIRED IN OBJECTIVES/PLAN
January		
February		
March		
April		
May		
June		
July		
August		
September		
October		
November		
December		

*This worksheet may be reproduced without further permission from the publisher.

STEP 4

HOW TO INTRODUCE THE PERSONAL PERFORMANCE CONTRACT

Employees should understand that a Personal Performance Contract, more than any other document, will educate them about how much they are needed. A carefully prepared PPC should emphasize:

- Improving product quality

- Streamlining operations

- Improving customer satisfaction

- Reducing accidents

- Upgrading efficiency

- Cutting downtime

- Increasing profits

- Developing markets

- Stimulating morale

or . . .

- Suggesting new ideas on ways trouble can be avoided

PPC's SHOULD MAKE EACH EMPLOYEE FEEL LIKE PART OF A WINNING TEAM

TIPS TO COMPLETE THE PPC

As you prepare to fill out a Personal Performance Contract with your employees, keep these guidelines in mind:

- Plan the meeting carefully

- Establish a friendly "we" atmosphere

- Ask the employee to participate by summarizing what she/he has prepared

- Encourage initiative

- Help employees keep contracts as simple, brief and clear as possible

- Insure results are measurable

- Get commitments (dates and schedules) from those involved

- Probe to insure that the objectives and action plans are realistic

- Summarize the expected results of each PPC

- Thank employees for participating and inform them you will be interested to track their progress

- Answer any questions

ELIMINATING OBJECTIONS

Often items will surface in a PPC that are likely to bring objections from the person reviewing the plan. When this is anticipated, an "objection-eliminator" worksheet should be prepared. A sample is shown on the facing page.

SAMPLE AHEAD

SAMPLE
OBJECTION-ELIMINATOR WORKSHEET

ITEM IN PPC THAT MAY RAISE QUESTIONS/ OBJECTIONS	SUPPORTING EVIDENCE	BENEFITS	PRESENTATION METHODS
Assign Ed Smith as assistant manager—accounts receivable.	Ed has more than 6 years experience in handling billing procedures (2 with us—4 with a competitor)	BENEFITS FOR BOSS Reduce overtime by 15% (estimated to save $2,300)	AUDIO
	He spent last 6 months setting up billing procedures with our computer staff	Eliminate need for outside help at end of each month (estimated to save $7,500)	VISUALS
	He wants to transfer & his present boss agrees	Decrease overdue accounts receivable (Estimated to save $2,800)	DOCUMENTS
	This job would be a logical promotion	BENEFITS FOR COMPANY	Show time sheets for last 6 months
	He should qualify as my replacement within 2 years or he could be promoted to the midwest division	Save up to $38,000 per year BENEFITS FOR CUSTOMERS	Mgmt. costs resulting from overtime and expenses from help brought in from outside
		Invoices received same time each month	STAFF
		Mistakes reduced by 10%	
		Prompt payors will not be subsidizing poor payors	OTHER Show letters of complaint from customers about late invoices

DO YOU OR YOUR EMPLOYEES HAVE
OBJECTIONS THAT NEED ELIMINATING?

IF SO, USE THE FORM ON THE FACING PAGE.

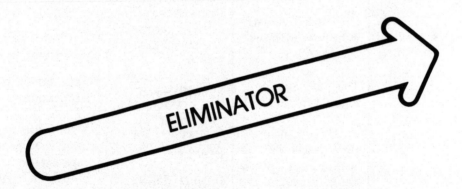

ELIMINATOR

OBJECTION-ELIMINATOR WORKSHEET*

ITEM IN PPC THAT MAY RAISE QUESTIONS/ OBJECTIONS	SUPPORTING EVIDENCE	BENEFITS	PRESENTATION METHODS
		BENEFITS FOR BOSS	AUDIO
			VISUALS
		BENEFITS FOR COMPANY	DOCUMENTS
			STAFF
		BENEFITS FOR CUSTOMERS	OTHER

*This sheet may be copied without further permission of the publisher.

STEP 5	# FOLLOWING THROUGH ON PERFORMANCE CONTRACTS

Nothing is completely predictable in life, and this includes performance contracts. Changes will occur, often with little or no advance warning.

Because of this uncertainty, PPC's need to be monitored on a regular, continuing basis.

Some people may become discouraged if their PPC and plan do not work out exactly as prepared. They forget that it is human to make mistakes and that plans–despite the checkpoints built into them–can fall short of the mark. There is no way to protect against <u>all</u> random events. That is part of the fun and challenge of life.

Therefore, when a PPC strays off-course, an opportunity exists to encourage your employees to not only determine what's wrong, but develop an action plan of what to do. One way to accomplish this is to ANALYZE all PPC's at least once a quarter.

The facing page provides a simple way to get things back on track.

CHECKPOINTS FOR ACTION

CHECKPOINT	WHAT TO ANALYZE	ACTIONS TO TAKE
Honestly review performance in relation to objectives defined in the performance contract	What was performance like before the PPC was developed? What is performance at this time? What could it be if PPC is fully realized?	Inspect previous performance evaluations Review current records Check PPC to see how well present performance measures up to objectives
Look for weaknesses	Check weak areas in relation to existing conditions, and determine who or what is the cause If outside assistance is needed, who should be told?	Monitor complaints, oversights, mistakes. Evaluate costs in terms of time lost, downtime, waste, etc. Determine key needs that demand satisfaction and resolve them
Keep an eye on time	Where are the time problems? Can they be accommodated within original PPC?	Pinpoint causes If timelines were not realistic; reset them to reflect reality
Identify management's needs, requirements and wants	What changes have occurred since the PPC was approved? Which activities/objectives in the PPC are currently of greatest importance to the organization?	Maintain strong communication to insure key individuals have current information Provide avenues for regular feedback from associates
Check the environment	What is new, unusual or different within markets served by your company? What effect do trends and changing patterns have on the PPC under review?	Read appropriate journals to understand conditions in markets served by the company. Track competition to know how they are doing in the same markets Adjust PPC as required to reflect environment
Determine what action needs to be taken	Organize, initiate and follow through on viable remaining items in PPC.	Revise PPC as required. Prioritize remaining projects to be accomplished. Decide what needs to be done, by whom and when. Assign accountabilitty for results. Set date for next review.

ASSURING TEAMWORK*

Normally a Personal Performance Contract and action plan will involve others. An employee may request your help, or you may see a need for it. That's when a <u>team</u> approach may be the best answer.

Before acting, however, you should first determine:

• Who must be involved?

• Why are they needed?

• What are the critical tasks for each person?

• Does each person know what is expected of him/her?

• Do team members know what is expected of other members?

• Is the team approach consistent with individual PPC's and objectives of the organization?

In situations requiring teamwork neither the extent of the problem nor the need for assistance can be accurately developed into an effective performance contract until the situation has been analyzed. The checklist on the facing page will help you decide how to follow through.

SITUATION ANALYSIS WORKSHEET ⟩

* For an excellent book on Team Building, see Robert Maddux's <u>Team Building: An Exercise in Leadership</u> listed on page 69.

SITUATION ANALYSIS WORKSHEET

1. <u>INVESTIGATE</u>

   ☐ What caused the situation?

   ☐ What has been learned about conditions surrounding the situation?

   ☐ Have notes been made of key points?

2. <u>EVALUATE</u>

   ☐ Has essential information been reviewed for accuracy?

   ☐ Have the key factors been isolated?

   ☐ Is there enough information to develop an action plan?

3. <u>RECORD</u>

   ☐ Can a statement be prepared summarizing the problem or situation?

   > What happened?
   > Who or what is affected?
   > Why did the situation develop?
   > How was the situation discovered?

4. <u>TAKE ACTION</u>

   ☐ Have alternatives been prepared or considered?

   ☐ What results are to be achieved (by whom? by when?)

   ☐ What is the extent of any losses?

   ☐ Has a date been established for follow-up review?

With information from a situation analysis worksheet, it should be possible to determine <u>WHO</u> is best qualified to help, and to <u>DETERMINE</u>:

- The type of assistance required.

- The available alternatives.

- The time, materials and people required.

- An estimate of the costs involved.

- How individual PPC's need to be revised to meet the reality of the new situation.

> The opportunity to work with others as part of a team should be a highly rewarding experience. It can enhance personal job skills, and also lead to new approaches which can generate renewed enthusiasm.

HOORAY FOR TEAMS

BENEFITS OF TEAMWORK

Perhaps the most important benefits of a legitimate team effort are the after-effects. A meeting with the team is an ideal time to review the situation, discuss the tactics used, and assess results that have been achieved. As you analyze the results together, this is an excellent opportunity to:

• Thank team members for what was accomplished.

• Ask where improvements could have been made.

• Identify obstacles that might affect future situations, and discuss alternatives for dealing with them.

• Solicit ideas for new objectives to incorporate into current performance contracts—and those which will be developed in the future.

Another significant advantage of working as a team lies in the increased knowledge and experience for individual team members. When a team approach works well, <u>everyone</u> in an organization benefits.

THE STEP-BY-STEP PROCESS

So far, we have emphasized creating a personal performance contract by deciding on the WHAT'S, HOW'S, and WHEN'S involved. Now it is time to become very practical. On the next page are 10 simple steps to follow to insure your PPC and those of your employees are what you want.

TEN-STEP CHECKLIST

CHECK ☑ EACH STEP AS IT IS COMPLETED.

	DOES MY BOSS AGREE?		
	YES	NO.	Why not?

☐   1.   Has the necessary information been assembled?   ___   ___   _____

☐   2.   Have the expected key results for the job been identified and listed?   ___   ___   _____

☐   3.   Have the greatest needs for each key result area been determined?   ___   ___   _____

☐   4.   Do I know why these needs are important and what result is expected for each?   ___   ___   _____

☐   5.   Have I ranked the importance of each result expected?   ___   ___   _____

☐   6.   Have I identified potential obstacles?   ___   ___   _____

☐   7.   Have I determined the most reasonable and realistic performance targets for each key result area?   ___   ___   _____

☐   8.   Do I know which measurement assessments are best (quality, quantity, time, cost)?   ___   ___   _____

☐   9.   Does my action plan adequately address accountability? (who will do what by when).   ___   ___   _____

☐   10.   Have I involved all key people who can affect the outcome?   ___   ___   _____

Personal Performance Contracts

CREATING COMMITMENT

What should the outcome be of a well written Personal Performance Contract? One immediate benefit should be a commitment to improve productivity.

Some experts believe a major reason for the decline in the "work ethic" is that many employees feel their jobs are boring or even dehumanizing. Others take less pride in what they do because they consider their work unfulfilling.

The Personal Performance Contract can be a major step in overcoming these problems. A thoughtful PPC should get people involved and make them feel they are making an important contribution. Becoming part of the action, and not a piece of machinery, will provide a sense of personal satisfaction.

A well done Personal Performance Contract will give employees a chance to accomplish more and to do it better. By involving employees, and working with them, it is possible to take advantage of the <u>pride</u> most want to feel for what they are doing. Perhaps most important of all, a good PPC can put enjoyment into what people are paid to do.

What it takes to develop a high quality PPC is <u>COMMITMENT</u>.

TO LEARN HOW A COMMITMENT CAN BE CREATED CHECK THE FACING PAGE.

STEPS TO CREATE JOB COMMITMENT

1. DEVELOP

   - Insure commitments are within the capabilities of each person.

   - Provide advice and direction to help structure meaningful commitments for your employees.

   - Set a good personal example by developing a quality Personal Performance Contract with <u>your</u> boss.

2. WEIGH

   - Determine how well the commitments in each PPC address the highest priority needs of the job at this time.

   - Assess how employee commitments support or reinforce those you have made on your PPC.

   - Evalute how realistic the PPC is relative to problems which stand in the way.

3. DISCUSS

   - Provide regular communication with those involved. Construct avenues for feedback.

   - Insure commitments of team members are communicated to everyone directly involved.

   - Determine accountability for all commitments.

4. UTILIZE

   - Encourage individuals to be innovative and develop new solutions.

   - Create opportunities to discuss actions taken, as well as obstacles encountered.

   - Analyze all projects or programs in trouble to determine why they are faltering and what can be done to save them.

| STEP 6 | THE FINAL STEP |

Now, it's time to put it all together. First, review the example on page 29. Then ask those involved to complete a PPC using the blank form on the facing page. Pencil should be used so changes can be made after discussion between you and each employee.

After revision (as often as it takes), a PPC will be ready for implementation when agreement is reached by you and the employee on it and the action plan required to carry it out.

Personal Performance Contracts

PERSONAL PERFORMANCE CONTRACT WORKSHEET*   FOR _____

NAME

Key Result Area	Need	Why Important	How Important %	Potential Obstacles	Performance Targets/Results Expected	Measures Quality/Quantity Time, Cost	Action Plan (Who, What, When)

*This worksheet may be photocopied without further permission from the publisher.

On the facing page is an example of a completed PPC. Notice that it follows the basic principles provided throughout this book.

–The key result areas are identified

–The objectives are stated clearly in terms of results expected

–Progress measures are indicated in terms of quantity, quality, time and cost

IT'S SHOWTIME!

SAMPLE PERFORMANCE CONTRACT

Date: _12/1/_

Location: _District Office_

To: _John Simpson:_ District Manager

From: _Beverly Jones:_ Local Manager

Within the period _1/1 — 3/31_ the following will be accomplished:

I Key Result Area _Service Center Expansion_

OBJECTIVE	Date
Open three new suburban service centers in Fairview, Newport and Mapleton and have them open for business by: Total average cost not to exceed previously established budget in each case.	3/15 Fairview 3/31 Newport 3/1 Mapleton

II Key Result Area _Recruiting/Placement_

OBJECTIVE	Date
Select a qualified service manager from within the company for each of above locations. Selection to be completed by:	2/1 Fairview 2/15 Newport 1/15 Mapleton

III Key Result Area _Training_

OBJECTIVE	Date
Train service manager for above new locations. Training content to be developed by: Training content to be approved by District Mgr. by: Training to take place by:	1/5 1/10 3/1 Fairview 3/15 Newport 2/15 Mapleton

You will be kept informed of the progress on each of these objectives at our weekly meetings.

I understand that meeting these objectives will be the most significant factors in my performance evaluation and compensation.

Beverly Jones
Local Manager signature

John Simpson
District Manager signature

PERSONAL PERFORMANCE CONTRACT

Date: _____

Location: _____

_____

To: _____

From: _____

Within the period _____ the following will be accomplished:

I Key Result Area _____

OBJECTIVE   Date

	Date

II Key Result Area _____

OBJECTIVE   Date

	Date

III Key Result Area _____

OBJECTIVE   Date

	Date

You will be kept informed of the progress on each of these objectives at our weekly meetings.

I understand that meeting these objectives will be significant factors in my performance evaluation and compensation.

_____

_____

64

WHAT HAVE YOU LEARNED?

Now it's time to check on what you have
learned. Answer each of the twenty questions
on the facing page. Answers are on page 66.
Give yourself five points for each correct answer.

MEASURE YOUR PROGRESS

It is time to review your
progress. There are twenty
statements on the facing
page. They are either true
or false. Each correct
answer is worth five points.

READING REVIEW

Please answer each of these questions true or false.

True   False

____ ____ 1. Performance Contracts should deal with the little things that you are likely to forget about if not put in writing.

____ ____ 2. Things which are easily accomplished make the best performance contracts.

____ ____ 3. The first step in preparing a PPC is to set objectives.

____ ____ 4. Accountability is determining <u>who</u> will do <u>what</u> by <u>when</u>

____ ____ 5. Your PPC should concentrate on high priorities which achieve significant results.

____ ____ 6. The PPC should be designed exclusively from the point of view of the employee.

____ ____ 7. The key to job success is planned, sustained effort.

____ ____ 8. Your strengths and weaknesses should be discussed with your boss when preparing your PPC.

____ ____ 9. Individual PPC's need not necessarily be related to company goals.

____ ____ 10. It's a good idea to use the PPC to measure every aspect of your job.

____ ____ 11. A key result area is the same as a goal.

____ ____ 12. Progress indicators are ways to measure goals.

____ ____ 13. Possible obstacles should be considered after your PPC has been agreed upon.

____ ____ 14. The PPC should be discussed when projects/objectives are completed.

____ ____ 15. The PPC is best introduced in a memo from the company president.

____ ____ 16. Questions and objections should normally be handled by writing them down and then meeting face-to-face to discuss them.

____ ____ 17. Personal Performance Contracts combine top down direction and bottom up participation.

____ ____ 18. PPC's should be prepared by you after your boss has decided on the problems you should solve.

____ ____ 19. In performance contracts the <u>whats</u> are more important than the <u>hows</u>.

____ ____ 20. The greatest benefits of PPC's are commitment and results.

66

ANSWERS TO QUESTIONS ON PAGE 65

1. False PPC's should be concerned with your most important responsibilities.

2. False Best results are achieved when extra effort is required.

3. False Unless we <u>analyze needs</u> first we may set objectives that are meaningless.

4. True

5. True Don't waste time on "flyspecks."

6. False <u>Both</u> boss and employee should be involved and agree on the final contract.

7. True To count on anything else is naive.

8. True Bosses can't read minds. Worse yet, he/she may guess wrong!

9. False Any PPC should directly relate to employer expectation and priorities.

10. False Measurement should be directed toward key result areas.

11. False Key result areas are the vital components of your job. It is from these that measurable goals can be constructed.

12. True They are usually best expressed in terms of quantity, quality, time and cost.

13. False Anticipation of potential obstacles can sharpen focus and save time.

14. False Progress should be reported and evaluated regularly.

15. False To be effective PPC's should be introduced personally by a supervisor.

16. True Writing tends to focus thinking but "memo wars" without personal contact can make things worse.

17. True It is this combination which enables managers to function most effectively.

18. False You should participate at all stages of the PPC.

19. True We must first be sure we are doing the right things, then concentrate on doing them right.

20. True Commitment determines persistence. Results (not activities) are what we are paid to achieve.

AUTHOR'S RESPONSE TO CASES

DIFFICULT CHOICES (page 13)

A. A PPC would provide a way to insure that Joe and Jim were working on the things that most needed to be done. They are drifting because: (1) expectations have not been clearly stated; (2) they are getting by with doing less; (3) Harry is reluctant to deal with them.

Working together on a PPC will help everyone become aware of the problems, and allow Harry to face the issue of reduced performance.

B. Key Results for Joe as a Production Supervisor should include:
—production targets and schedules
—manpower targets and schedules
—quality control guidelines
—cost control targets...etc.

C. As Engineering Supervisor, Jim's key results areas could include:
—preventive maintenance goals
—construction contract targets
—contractor relations guidelines
—equipment design specifications
—machine operating standards...etc.

D. No more than six months to show positive results. Thoughtful PPC's can help. If they do not; Harry Phillips should be taken out of his managerial position.

WHAT WOULD YOU DO? (pg 31)

A. Sue is likely to find herself doing more and more of Mary's work.

B. Mary may think, ''What a great boss I've got.'' Without realizing it, however, she is retarding her own development. She won't grow until she accepts accountability for her work.

C. It is Sue's responsibility as supervisor to take action. She should: (1) stop doing Mary's work; (2) tell her why; (3) help Mary develop a PPC which will incorporate her most important duties in measurable ways; (4) hold Mary to the terms of the contract.

D. We don't know much about Mary's ability, but a PPC should be prepared by Mary (with Sue's help) using the procedures outlined in this book.

VOLUNTARY CONTRACT

Even completing this book may require a personal performance contract of sorts. Why not consider making a contract with a supervisor, or friend to complete this book to the best of your ability? If you believe a contract would help, use the form on the facing page.

VOLUNTARY
CONTRACT*

I, _____ , hereby agree
(Your name)

to meet with the individual designated below within

thirty days to discuss my progress toward constructing a

Personal Performance Contract. The purpose of this meeting

will be to *review* areas of strength and establish action steps for

areas where improvement may still be required.

_____
Signature

I agree to meet with the above individual on

_____
Month   *Date*   *Time*

at the following location.

_____

_____
Signature

*The purpose of this agreement is to motivate you to incorporate
concepts and techniques of this program into your daily
activities. It also provides a degree of accountability between
you and the person you select to sign the agreement.

NOTES

FOR OTHER FIFTY-MINUTE SELF-STUDY BOOKS
SEE THE BACK OF THIS BOOK.

NOTES

FOR OTHER FIFTY-MINUTE SELF-STUDY BOOKS
SEE THE BACK OF THIS BOOK.

NOTES

FOR OTHER FIFTY-MINUTE SELF-STUDY BOOKS
SEE THE BACK OF THIS BOOK.

NOTES

FOR OTHER FIFTY-MINUTE SELF-STUDY BOOKS
SEE THE BACK OF THIS BOOK.

NOTES

FOR OTHER FIFTY-MINUTE SELF-STUDY BOOKS
SEE THE BACK OF THIS BOOK.

NOTES

FOR OTHER FIFTY-MINUTE SELF-STUDY BOOKS
SEE THE BACK OF THIS BOOK.

FOR OTHER FIFTY-MINUTE SELF-STUDY BOOKS
SEE THE BACK OF THIS BOOK.

ABOUT THE FIFTY-MINUTE SERIES

We hope you enjoyed this book and found it valuable. If so, we have good news for you. This title is part of the best selling *FIFTY-MINUTE Series* of books. All other books are similar in size and identical in price. Several books are supported with a training video. These are identified by the symbol **Ⓥ** next to the title.

Since the first *FIFTY-MINUTE* book appeared in 1986, more than five million copies have been sold worldwide. Each book was developed with the reader in mind. The result is a concise, high quality module written in a positive, readable self-study format.

FIFTY-MINUTE Books and Videos are available from your distributor or from Crisp Publications, Inc., 95 First Street, Los Altos, CA 94022. A free current catalog is available on request.

The complete list of *FIFTY-MINUTE Series* Books and Videos are listed on the following pages and organized by general subject area.

MANAGEMENT TRAINING (Cont.)

PERSONNEL/HUMAN RESOURCES

COMMUNICATIONS

CUSTOMER SERVICE/SALES TRAINING (CONT.)

SMALL BUSINESS/FINANCIAL PLANNING

ADULT LITERACY/BASIC LEARNING

CAREER BUILDING

To order books/videos from the FIFTY-MINUTE Series, please:

1. **CONTACT YOUR DISTRIBUTOR**

   or

2. **Write to Crisp Publications, Inc.**
   95 First Street   (415) 949-4888 - phone
   Los Altos, CA 94022   (415) 949-1610 - FAX